MW00778761

SHOWDOWN
With the Devil

Chapter 1
SATAN'S IMITATION

A dictionary definition of the word "supernatural" is as follows:

(1) Existing or occurring outside the normal experience or knowledge of man. Not explainable by the known forces or laws of nature. Involving or attributed to God.

(2) Involving or attributed to ghosts, spirits, the occult, etc.

(3) Exceeding the normal bounds we understand.

I was happy to see that the person who wrote that definition attributed supernatural power to God, but also recognized that Satan has supernatural power.

Many people today are in bondage to the *false* flow of the supernatural. But there's a *real* supernatural power in the world, too, and I call it the super-supernatural. (I picked up that phrase from John Osteen, who wrote a book by that title: *How To Flow in the Super Supernatural.*)

There has been a rapid expansion of Satan's supernatural power in our world today. The kingdom of darkness has spread throughout every level of society. We see it in the newspaper. We see it on television. We listen to it on the radio. And it's happening all over the world: People who are genuinely searching for the supernatural are being led astray by the enemy.

People are seeking information and help through witchcraft, sorcery, and the false religions. They even welcome counsel from psychic mediums and others who are clairvoyant. We read in the newspapers and see on television all the time how certain police departments have gone to clairvoyants and mediums to solve cases, and it's a known fact that some have been able to solve cases. Why? The devil will reveal his supernatural power if he can trap some people.

You see, the enemy has substituted his false supernatural for God's super-supernatural. That's why people are turning to fortune-telling, Ouija boards, witchcraft, black magic, Eastern religions, seances, palmistry, numerology, Satan worship, Tarot cards, crystal ball gazing, and astrology (interpreting the signs of the zodiac).

There's also necromancy, the practice of talking with the spirits of the dead; but the latest and most popular occult practice is astral projection, the art of projecting oneself out of the body by the power of demonic spirits. The people involved think this psychic phenomenon is accomplished through supernatural power, but it is not the true supernatural power of God; it is Satan's false supernatural power.

Chapter 2
CHRISTIANS AND ASTROLOGY

Astrology is especially popular today. The signs of the zodiac are all around us. Many Christians have astrology books in their homes and wear the signs of the zodiac as charms on bracelets or necklaces and don't even realize what they're doing. Many consult their newspaper's astrology column everyday to see what's going to happen under their "sign."

Quit playing around with the enemy! Shun the very appearance of evil!

Some will say, "Oh, you don't know what you're talking about."

My reply is that God's Word is very clear in its warning against the false supernatural, which is energized by Satan himself.

The Book of Deuteronomy is a condensation of all that's in the first four books of the law. This is what it says about occult (Satanic) practices:

DEUTERONOMY 18:10–14 (*Amplified*)
10 There shall not be found among you anyone
who makes his son or daughter pass through the
fire, or who uses divination, or is a soothsayer, or
an augur, or a sorcerer,
11 Or a charmer, or a medium, or a wizard, or a
necromancer.
12 For all who do these things are an abomination
to the Lord, and it is because of these abominable
practices that the Lord your God is driving them
[the Canaanites] out before you.
13 You shall be blameless [and absolutely true] to
the Lord your God.
14 For these nations whom you shall dispossess
listen to soothsayers and diviners. But as for you,
the Lord your God has not allowed you to do so.

(A soothsayer is a fortune-teller. An augur
predicts the future from omens. A necromancer talks with the spirits of the dead.)

This passage is stated in very clear language. Another Old Testament reference to
the occult is when the Lord spoke to Moses
and said, *"Ye shall keep my sabbaths, and
reverence my sanctuary: I am the Lord. Re-
gard not them that have familiar spirits,
neither seek after wizards, to be defiled by
them . . ."* (Lev. 19:30–31).

6

These evil practices also are mentioned in the New Testament. For example, John says, *"Little children, keep yourselves from idols"* (1 John 5:21).

Recently I heard a radio news report that a palm-reader took $16,000 from some people to deliver them from demons. (Sometimes the devil will relieve his own demonic power from people for a while to make believers out of them. In such cases it's evil demonstrating the supernatural.)

Many people never have realized that Satan's power is strong. He does have supernatural power! All you have to do is take a trip to Haiti to realize this. They practice a great deal of voodoo, communicating in trances with evil spirits, etc. Or go into many areas in the Far East and in Africa and you'll see demonic powers in operation. That's why you don't have any trouble getting those people to believe in the supernatural, because they have been involved with the false supernatural all of their lives.

They have seen people walk on live coals of fire and not be burned. They have seen people lie on beds of nails and be unharmed. They have seen all kinds of manifestations of the supernatural power of the enemy.

And when you come in with the true supernatural power of God and demonstrate that His power is greater than the false, demonic power they are acquainted with, they'll turn aside and follow the real power of God.

We believers have been so naive, clustering in our little churches, that we have not realized that the world is crying for the super-supernatural power of God, yet they're being deceived by the enemy's false supernatural power.

One reason the world is being deceived is because we talk about the supernatural power of God, but we don't *demonstrate* it. And the main reason why most people don't demonstrate the supernatural is because they don't have any boldness and they won't step out.

Meanwhile, the great flood of satanic influence is beginning to engulf the society in which we live. We would do well to remember what Jesus said in Matthew:

8

MATTHEW 24:24
24 For there shall arise false Christs, and false prophets, and shall shew great signs and wonders; insomuch that, if it were possible, they shall deceive the very elect.

The Church is the elect. Thank God, He has given us the Holy Spirit that we might demonstrate the true supernatural power of God. The only true supernatural—the only real satisfaction from the supernatural —comes from the baptism of the Holy Spirit and the operation of the gifts of the Spirit.

But those who practice idolatry, witchcraft, hatred, and all the other works of the devil will have no place in the kingdom of God, according to Galatians 5:20–21. The Book of Revelation is also clear about the end of those who practice the occult:

REVELATION 21:8
8 But the fearful, and unbelieving, and the abominable, and murderers, and whoremongers, and sorcerers, and idolaters, and all liars, shall have their part in the lake which burneth with fire and brimstone: which is the second death.

Chapter 3
SHOWDOWN WITH THE DEVIL

Joel prophesied regarding the great outpouring of the supernatural that is coming upon the earth in the last days. Peter quoted this prophecy in Acts:

ACTS 2:17–19
17 And it shall come to pass in the last days, saith God, I will pour out of my Spirit upon all flesh: and your sons and your daughters shall prophesy, and your young men shall see visions, and your old men shall dream dreams:
18 And on my servants and on my handmaidens I will pour out in those days of my Spirit; and they shall prophesy:
19 And I will shew wonders in heaven above, and signs in the earth beneath; blood, and fire, and vapour of smoke.

Friends, we are headed for a showdown with the devil in these last days. If you don't believe that the enemy has supernatural power, go back to the Old Testament and read how Pharaoh's wizards and wisemen did some of the same miracles Moses did when he appeared before Pharaoh and demanded the deliverance of the children of Israel. But you'll also find out that the super-supernatural power of God will always go one step further.

I remember my Dad telling about going to a meeting one time with another minister. Supernatural phenomena were occurring, and many good people were being taken in, but the two ministers recognized that the source of this power was demonic. The speaker was using familiar spirits as the source of his knowledge, but the people thought this was the operation of the word of knowledge. That's what familiar spirits do; they operate much the same as the word of knowledge.

My Dad and his friend began to use the Name of Jesus. All of a sudden nothing could happen. The man conducting the meeting finally said, "Unless those two gentlemen sitting back there leave, I can't operate." The crowd got restless and wanted them out, because they thought the speaker was operating in the true supernatural realm.

We must realize that Satan has tried to produce a counterfeit for everything God has. I have talked to rock 'n' roll performers, and they told me when they get on the platform and begin to sing, something comes over them, takes over, and gives them a supernatural rapport with that audience. You see, that's the devil's counterfeit of what happens to the minister of the Gospel.

There is power there in that rock concert, but that power is not stronger than the power of God!

ISAIAH 59:19
19 . . .When the enemy shall come in like a flood, the Spirit of the Lord shall lift up a standard against him.

The Spirit of God is raising up a standard against Satan's demonic powers through the mighty baptism of the Holy Spirit and the power of God. Like a sleeping giant, the Church, which has been slumbering in self-complacency, is shaking itself, realizing the truth of God's power.

In the past some have been jumping and

clapping in church on one hand and reading their horoscope in the newspaper on the other to see what their day was going to be like.

I can tell you what *my* day is going to be like today, tomorrow, and the next day, and the next day, if Jesus tarries. I don't have to get a certain star in a certain position or have the planet Mercury and the planet Venus involved in orbit with something else. *My* day is going to be a great day!

But many good church people, without realizing it, are giving place to the devil through such practices as astrology, talking about what "sign" they're born under. Bless God, *I'm born under the sign of the cross, the blood of the Lord Jesus Christ!*

That's the only sign that means anything! The only sign that has delivering power is the cross, through the blood Jesus shed on it. That cross is a place of death—it represents death—*but the blood that flowed from that cross represents life—supernaturally.*

As I was sitting in my office, working on this message, I began to see that man-made tradition is melting like the snow. The walls of tradition and theology are not strong enough to hold those who are looking for the super-supernatural.

When the Lord gave me that thought, I jumped up and danced a little. I started thinking about God's people rising like the dawn over the earth and marching to the drumbeat of God's triumphant song. This "awakening generation," as John Osteen calls it, is climbing the hill of God to get above the muck and the mire and the smog and the fog of tradition and sectarianism; they are seeking the super-supernatural.

We are overcomers in Christ Jesus! Greater is He that is in me than he that is in the world! No weapon formed against me can prosper!

There may be demonic supernatural phenomena happening all around me, but I will demonstrate the true supernatural power of God to this searching generation.

Chapter 4
TRUSTING IN THE SUPERNATURAL

You'll find out how much you rely on the super-supernatural when you're stranded with a friend in the East African bush, surrounded by a pile of your luggage, and night is fast approaching.

We had landed nearby on a grassy strip when the pilot couldn't land the little single-engine plane where he was supposed to.

Natives were going to and fro along the road. I couldn't understand their language, and they couldn't understand mine. Evangelist Mark Brazee, a RHEMA graduate, was with me. I said, "Mark, what are we going to do?"

He said, "The only thing I know to do is try to hitch a ride." We had seen tiny taxicabs in that country, so we decided to wait for one to come along. The shadows deepened.

A girl approached. My attention was drawn to her before she got close to us. My spirit on the inside knew something was going to happen.

When the girl got almost parallel with us, she turned, pointed, and began to scream and jabber. I immediately recognized the devil in her. Faces began to appear from behind every tree and bush, it seemed.

I looked at Mark and he looked at me. He was waiting for me to act, because I was the spiritual "leader"!

I grabbed hold of Mark's hand and prayed, "In the Name of Jesus!" The supernatural power of Jesus is stronger than the supernatural power of the enemy. The girl stopped screaming and walked on down the road. Everybody left.

Before leaving for that trip, I had turned myself over to the supernatural power of God. It's a good thing I had, because after arriving in Africa we did the most dangerous thing we could possibly have done: We looked up a taxi driver and hired him to take us 110 kilometers to our speaking engagement.

When Brother Silas Owiti heard this, he

called his people together, and they got down on their knees and began to pray. This was on a Saturday evening. We had to preach Sunday in this other town; that's why we were trying so hard to get there.

We got into that taxi and headed out. I had not been to bed since leaving Tulsa on Thursday morning. I was exhausted. I went to sleep in the taxi, waking up several times. It was raining so hard I don't know how the driver kept the car on the road. We were hitting bumps and sliding all over. But I was sleeping in the arms of the Holy Spirit. You see, I believe in the supernatural power of God taking care of me.

We found out later that taking a taxi was the worst thing we could possibly have done. Brother Silas told me, "A lot of those taxi drivers are the bad element. All the time they take people from other countries out in the jungle in the middle of the night, kill them, take all of their belongings, and nobody finds their bodies for weeks and months."

Another supernatural act that happened

to us in Africa concerned our camera. We left it on the seat of the taxi. Everybody said it was gone forever. Brother Silas sent one of his workers back to town, but everyone agreed it would be doubtful that he could even find that taxi driver. I said, "He'll find him and he'll get the camera."

The man returned with the camera. That was a supernatural miracle of God.

I want you to realize that Jesus is the absolute Master of three worlds: Heaven, earth, and the region of darkness. *The enemy has only as much power as we allow him to have.* We can stop him whenever we desire.

Once you understand what the Word of God has to say about defeating Satan, you will never again be afraid of his false supernatural power or of using the super-supernatural power of God to defeat him.

You see, the super-supernatural power is the clothing or armor God gives His people to destroy the works of the enemy. Just as we put on different clothing for the different times of the year as protection for the body, so the supernatural is the coat of power that God gives us to wear.

I like my clothing to be clean and precisely pressed. When I was in the Army, I'd put on that green serge uniform and make sure it was exactly right. And when I marched out, my head was high, my shoulders were back, my cap was just exactly the way it should be—and I walked with a spring in my step.

When I took that green serge Army coat to the cleaners, they dipped it in cleaning fluid to remove all the bacteria and dirt that had gotten entwined in the fibers.

I make sure I take equally good care of the armor of God—the supernatural coat of the power of God. I make sure it is well tailored. I make sure there are no wrinkles or spots on it. I make sure I put it on with pride. And I make sure it's exactly right.

I get in the prayer closet and clean it thoroughly. When I begin to pray, the power of God begins to flood through me. When I walk out of that prayer closet, I'm ready to meet the enemy on any level; any position.

Our victory comes through the supernatural. You can talk about victory all you want, but let's start *demonstrating* it with the supernatural.

Chapter 5
THE COMING
SUPERNATURAL REVIVAL

I came through the great Healing Revival of 1947–58. I have seen the supernatural power of God lift people out of chairs and off stretchers. I have seen tremendous moves of the supernatural power of God. Some of you, too, went to those huge tents that held 20,000 people, and you saw the miracles of healing.

I also have witnessed the move from the Healing Revival to the Revival of the Word. My heart is stirred to realize that you and I have lived to see the decade of the '80s.

Now we must combine the supernatural power of God and the Word of God for a last-day supernatural explosive revival for God!

Why? Because Jesus is coming! And the Word of God says that in the last days the enemy would rise up stronger and stronger, and false prophets and false teachers also would rise up, but we who know the truth of the supernatural power of God would rise up to defeat Satan every time he turned around!

Too many people want to play around with the devil and play around with God, too, and it doesn't work that way. We either have to sell out to God or forget it.

Too many people are playing church. They want all of the benefits and none of the work! They want to repeat all of the clichés and make all the fancy confessions, but they don't want to pay the price for what it takes to have the supernatural power of God at work in this earth.

Some will ask, "What do you mean, 'pay the price'?"

I'm talking about getting on your face before God, straightening up your life, and starting to live the lifestyle that's becoming to a child of God. No, I'm not preaching dos and don'ts; I'm preaching a lifestyle that God talks about in His Word.

I could care less about people's traditions: whether you've got on long sleeves or short sleeves, or whether or not you're wearing makeup. *That has nothing to do with spirituality—nothing!*

I will say this, however: If you clean up the man on the inside, he'll clean up the man on the outside! No, I didn't say you had to conform to somebody's rules and regulations; that's a lot of nonsense.

I was preaching in a certain town recently, and somebody came down to the front and said to me, "Hey—you take off that jewelry and God will fill you with the Holy Ghost!"

I said, "I got the Holy Ghost, jewelry and all. Go home. You're out of order."

You say, "That's awfully bold."

Let me tell you something: It's time that the Church of the Lord Jesus Christ got a little bold and demonstrated some supernatural power of God!

Some will say, "You're going around offending people."

I'll tell you what: Those kind need to be offended, because they're doing more harm to the kingdom of God than anybody else.

There are people in the church who are cry-babies, filled with unbelief and a lot of old tradition. And if the pastor or preacher tries to straighten them out, everybody sympathizes with them, saying, "Oh, you poor old dear. Why, they're just jumping all over you!"

I'd rather have a church full of people who smoke, drink, and take dope than a bunch like that, because then when I preached the truth of God's Word, they would see the error of their ways and I could bring them into the kingdom. People who are filled with manmade traditions are usually unteachable.

Chapter 6
EXERCISING
SPIRITUAL AUTHORITY

It's time we arose and began to demonstrate the supernatural power of God. Although we realize that the enemy has power, we also must realize that we've been giving him too much credit.

It seems like somebody is always giving a testimony about what the devil has done. You hear more about what the devil has done to them than what God has done. They spend 30 minutes telling you what the devil has done and take five minutes to tell you how God delivered them.

I'm only interested in the devil for one purpose, and that is to do what the Word of God says to do to him. The Word says I should step on him, tromp on him, and walk over the top of him.

Jesus said, *"All power is given unto me in heaven and in earth"* (Matt. 28:18). Actually, the word "power" should read "authority": "All *authority* is given unto me . . . ."

Jesus gave His authority to the Church. To do what? TO TREAD ON THE POWER OF THE ENEMY! The Apostle Paul put it this way: *"For he hath put all things under his feet"* (1 Cor. 15:27). What things? Supernatural things.

You need to exercise your spiritual authority, too, by getting rid of any occult items you've got around your house.

"Oh, So-and-so gave me that statue," some will argue.

If it is connected with any occult practices, get rid of it! Or if you've got any books about astrology (the signs of the zodiac) or other occult practices, GET RID OF THEM! DON'T GIVE ANY PLACE TO THE ENEMY!

Many will argue, "Oh, I don't believe in it anyway. I just read my horoscope to see what's going on."

You're giving place to the enemy. And if you're not careful, the enemy will find a place in your life.

"Oh, Brother Ken, I don't know . . . ."

Every time somebody preaches against

what the Bible calls sin, you say, "Oh, Brother, I don't know. I don't believe it's like that. I don't see it like that. I. . .I`. . .I."

Get the "I" out of the way and start talking about doing what the Word of God says, and you'll see the supernatural. You may be longing for the supernatural to move in your life, but "I" is in the way. Get "I" out of the way, and let the power of God move.

Do you really want the super-supernatural? You can have it. It's up to you; it's not up to God. It's not up to anybody but you. It depends on whether or not you want to pay the price to have the super-supernatural in your life.

Do you know that there are people who will live, die, and go to Heaven all without ever experiencing the super-supernatural power of God in their lives simply because they are not willing to pay the price? I didn't say they might not get to Heaven; I said they would not experience the super-supernatural. Oh, they might even operate in some of the gifts of the Spirit, but *carnality will never allow you to experience the super-supernatural.*

Our problem is that we talk about how carnal the Corinthian Church was, yet we never have stopped to look at the 20th century charismatic Church. *It is as carnal— or more so—than those Corinthians ever thought about being.*

Let's get rid of the carnality. Let's begin to live a lifestyle that's pleasing to God, and we'll see the super-supernatural.

We're rising. There is a group of us who are rising upon the horizon to demonstrate the super-supernatural power of God to this generation. And it's up to you whether or not you get involved in the Supernatural Revival. It's your decision, not mine. I've "laid it on the line" to you. Now it's up to you. What are you going to do?

Some of you have been giving place to the devil by the music you've been listening to, by some of the things you've been reading, by some of the things you've been viewing, and by some of the things you've been wearing. (Some of you who read this read your horoscope every day in the newspaper.)

If you are willing to pay the price to have

the super-supernatural operate in your life,
pray this with me:

Prayer: *Father, You know that I need to
change some things in my life. Even though
I know Jesus and I know the power of God, I
still need to change some things. I am going
to change, in the Name of Jesus. Amen.*